See Them Grow

DOG

by Dawn Bluemel Oldfield

Consultant: Kirsten Cooke, DVM
Diplomate, American College of Veterinary Internal Medicine
College of Veterinary Medicine
University of Florida
Gainesville, Florida

BEARPORT
PUBLISHING

New York, New York

Credits

Cover, © Eric Isselee/Shutterstock and © romakoma/Shutterstock; Title Page, © Happy monkey/Shutterstock; TOC, © Taigi/Shutterstock, © gilotyna4/Shutterstock, and © remik44992/Shutterstock; 4–5, © Chalabala/iStock; 6T, Kim Jones; 6–7, © steamroller_blues/Shutterstock; 8, Kim Jones; 9, Kim Jones; 10–11, Kim Jones; 12, © Brberrys/Shutterstock; 13, © Stock Connection Blue/Alamy; 14, © Jane Burton/NPL/Minden; 15, © Adriano Bacchella/NPL/Minden; 16, © Hannamariah/Shutterstock; 17, © schubbel/Shutterstock; 18T, © Viorel Sima/Shutterstock; 18B, © Alta Oosthuizen/Shutterstock; 19, © GROSSEMY VANESSA/Alamy; 20–21, © Mark Raycroft/Minden; 21R, © Eric Isselee/Shutterstock; 22T, © Henri Faure/Shutterstock; 22B, © Igor Normann/Shutterstock, © gilotyna4/Shutterstock, and © remik44992/Shutterstock; 23 (T to B), © Dora Zett/Shutterstock, © Isselee/Dreamstime, © Anna Hoychuk/Shutterstock, © steamroller_blues/Shutterstock, and © Africa Studio/Shutterstock; 24, © remik44992/Shutterstock.

Publisher: Kenn Goin
Editor: Jessica Rudolph
Creative Director: Spencer Brinker
Design: Debrah Kaiser
Photo Researcher: Thomas Persano

Library of Congress Cataloging-in-Publication Data

Names: Bluemel Oldfield, Dawn.
Title: Dog / by Dawn Bluemel Oldfield.
Description: New York, New York : Bearport Publishing, 2017. | Series: See them grow | Includes bibliographical references and index. | Audience: Ages 5 to 8.
Identifiers: LCCN 2016038816 (print) | LCCN 2016049925 (ebook) | ISBN 9781684020430 (library) | ISBN 9781684020959 (ebook)
Subjects: LCSH: Dogs—Growth—Juvenile literature.
Classification: LCC SF426.5 .B55 2017 (print) | LCC SF426.5 (ebook) | DDC 636.7—dc23
LC record available at https://lccn.loc.gov/2016038816

For more information, write to Bearport Publishing Company, Inc., 45 West 21st Street, Suite 3B, New York, New York 10010. Printed in the United States of America.

10 9 8 7 6 5 4 3 2 1

Contents

Dog

Woof, woof!

A Labrador retriever runs after its favorite toy.

The dog has a furry body, floppy ears, and a long tail.

How did it get this way?

There are more than 300 **breeds** of dogs, in many different sizes and colors.

A dog starts its life as a tiny **embryo.**

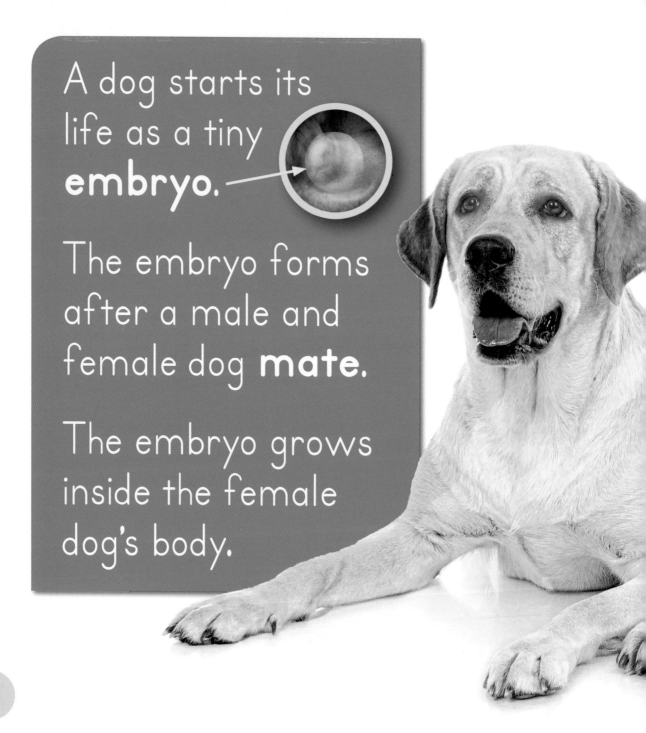

The embryo forms after a male and female dog **mate.**

The embryo grows inside the female dog's body.

The male dog of a breed is usually larger than the female dog.

The embryo grows quickly.

By one month, the tiny creature's eyes and legs start to form.

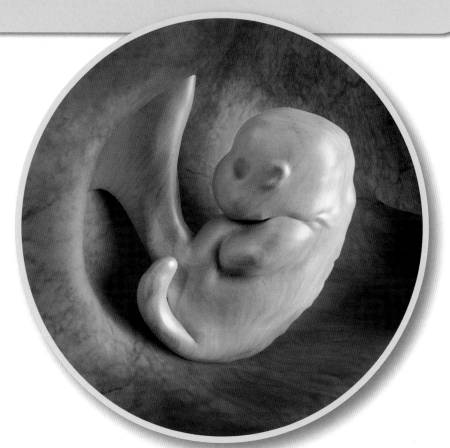

Its snout and paws take shape, too.

The embryo is about the size of a dime.

Inside the mother's body, the baby grows bigger every day.

By seven weeks, its body is covered in fur.

It looks like a tiny dog.

The baby gets **nutrients** from the mother's body through a cord connected to its belly button.

The mother dog's belly gets very big.

There are many puppies inside her.

By nine weeks, the mother is ready to give birth.

She has a **litter** of eleven puppies!

Small dog breeds have just a few puppies in a litter. Large breeds like Labradors have about seven puppies, but may have more.

13

A newborn Labrador is very small.

It weighs only about 1 pound (0.5 kg).

Its eyes and ears are closed, and it can't walk.

The tiny pup uses its senses of touch and smell to find its mother.

It crawls to her and drinks her milk.

Newborn puppies make soft squeaking sounds.

15

When the puppy is around two weeks old, its eyes and ears open.

It can start to see and hear for the first time!

Around this time, the puppy's first teeth come in. They are very sharp!

The puppy explores its surroundings.

It gets to know people and other animals.

17

When it's about four weeks old, the puppy is walking and running.

At first, its legs are wobbly, but the pup quickly grows strong.

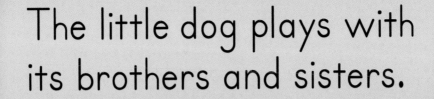

The little dog plays with its brothers and sisters.

When puppies reach 8 to 12 weeks old, many become part of a human family.

The puppy grows fast.

It will be fully grown in one to two years.

Soon it can have puppies of its own!

One of the smallest dog breeds is the Chihuahua (chih-WAH-wah). One of the largest is the Great Dane.

Dog Facts

❊ The average dog lives for about 10 to 14 years.

❊ The fastest dog is the greyhound. It can run 45 miles (72 km) an hour!

❊ All dogs have a much stronger sense of smell than humans. Breeds like beagles and basset hounds have the strongest sense of smell.

beagle

Glossary

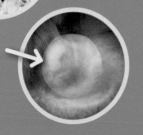 **breeds** (BREEDZ) kinds of dogs

 **embryo** (EM-bree-oh) an animal in the first stage of development

 **litter** (LIT-ur) a group of baby animals, such as puppies, that are born to the same mother at the same time

 **mate** (MAYT) to come together to have young

nutrients (NOO-tree-uhnts) substances needed by animals to grow and stay healthy

Index

Read More

Royston, Angela. *Life Cycle of a Dog.* Chicago: Heinemann (2009).

Schuetz, Kari. *Baby Dogs (Blastoff Readers: Super Cute).* Minneapolis, MN: Bellwether (2014).

Learn More Online

To learn more about dogs, visit
www.bearportpublishing.com/SeeThemGrow

About the Author

Dawn Bluemel Oldfield enjoys writing, reading, traveling, and gardening. She and her husband live in Prosper, Texas, and share their home with a big dog, a Siberian husky named McKenna, and one fabulous cat.